You, Too, Can Know Jesus

Jesus has lots
and lots
of friends.
He can be
your friend too!

Jesus is my very best friend.
He takes care of me,
just like He took care
of people in the Bible.

Jesus knew this little girl was very, very sick.
He went to visit her and made her well again.

Jesus can make us well
when we are sick.
He takes care of us
in many different ways,
and He wants to be our friend.
Would you like Jesus to be your
very best friend?

When Jesus lived on the
earth, He told people how
much God loves everyone.
God wants us to love
other people,
but sometimes
we do things to other people
that aren't very loving.
That is called sin.
Sin makes it hard for us
to be friends with God.

But because Jesus
loves us very much,
He died on the cross
to take the punishment
for all our sins.
When He takes away
our sins, we can be
close to God again!

Three days after Jesus died,
He came back alive!
Now He lives in heaven
with God,
but He still wants
to be our very best friend.

If you've never asked Jesus
to be your very best friend,
you can now.
All you need to do is
tell Him the wrong things
you have done,
say you are sorry, and
ask Him to forgive you.
Then you can ask Jesus to be
your very best friend.
And He will be—forever!

You can do that by praying a prayer like this one:

Dear Jesus,
thank You for showing us
how much You love us.
Please forgive me for all the
wrong things I have done.
Please be my very
best friend.
In Your name.
Amen.

Now that Jesus is your very
best friend, you can get to
know Him better.
You can do that by talking to
other people who are
friends of Jesus, and
by reading about Him
in the Bible.

Jesus is my very best friend.
I'm glad He's your friend too!

This is how God showed his love among us: He sent his one and only Son into the world that we might live through him.

I John 4:9

The best friend anyone can have is Jesus. *You, Too, Can Know Jesus*, tells children simply and clearly how they, too, can know Jesus and find Him as their very best friend!

Chariot Books™ is an imprint of David C. Cook Publishing Co.
David C. Cook Publishing Co., Elgin, Illinois 60120
David C. Cook Publishing Co., Weston, Ontario
Nova Distribution Ltd., Newton Abbot, England

You, Too, Can Know Jesus
© 1992 by David C. Cook for text and illustrations

All rights reserved. Except for brief excerpts for review purposes, no part of this book may be reproduced or used in any form without written permission from the publisher.
Written by Sue Leaf
Designed by Dawn Lauck and Mark Novelli
First Printing, 1992
Printed in the United States of America
96 95 94 93 92 5 4 3 2 1
LC 92-071782

Value Taught: Salvation
Ages 3-8

ISBN 0-7814-0920-9
99200

9 780781 409209